CW00406143

A FOREIGNER'S GUIDE TO MOSCOW

A Different Perspective

Elizabeth Barrett

The Book Guild Ltd
Sussex, England

First published in Great Britain in 2004 by
The Book Guild Ltd
25 High Street
Lewes, East Sussex
BN7 2LU

Copyright © Elizabeth Barrett 2004

The right of Elizabeth Barrett to be identified as the author of
this work has been asserted by her in accordance with the
Copyright, Designs and Patents Act 1988.

All rights reserved. No part of this publication may be reproduced, transmitted, or stored in a
retrieval system, in any form or by any means, without permission in writing from the publisher, nor
be otherwise circulated in any form of binding or cover other than that in which it is published and
without a similar condition being imposed on the subsequent purchaser.

Typesetting by
MRM Graphics Ltd

Printed and bound in Singapore under the supervision of
MRM Graphics Ltd, Winslow, Bucks

A catalogue record for this book is available from
The British Library.

ISBN 1 85776 852 3

CONTENTS

A Foreign View of Moscow

Contrary to popular western belief,
Moscow is not a drab, grey and lifeless city
with faceless Soviet architecture,
but is a vibrant city full of colour,
- bright, garish colours
and subtle pastel shades, -
with great architectural
variety and character.

I hope this assortment of
personal photographs
goes some way to correcting
misconceptions and
inspiring interest in the city.

To Muscovites:
Thank you for your hospitality.
No offence is intended by the
foreign humour.

LANDMARKS

St Basil's Cathedral,
– Moscow's most familiar landmark

Easy to recognise even when half cut

St Basil's and Red Square are popular with Muscovites at night . . .

. . . and by day

Red Square is popular with visitors . . .

. . . particularly tour groups

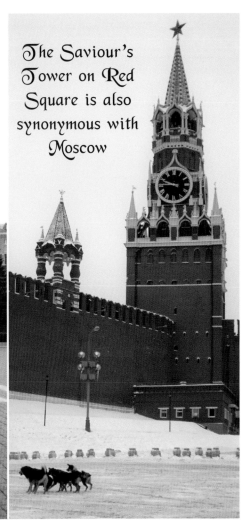

The Saviour's Tower on Red Square is also synonymous with Moscow

Lenin's mausoleum on Red Square: Why the guards, – to prevent his escape?

The rebuilt Kazan Cathedral:
different day, different d . . . oors and windows

A little-known entrance
to Red Square has
an ornate historical archway

The right steeple is thinner than the left

The rebuilt Resurrection
Gate to Red Square is best
seen from above ground level
– a viewing platform is provided

When visiting Moscow, it is a good idea
to carry a replica of St Basil's Cathedral
around with you

The silhouettes of St Basil's and the Saviour's Tower make it easy
to find one's way around Red Square in the smog . . .
(this about midday in The Great Smog of 2002)

Where are we?

. . . but it is too much for some

*Statue of Minin
and Pozharsky,
Red Square*

The Cathedral of Christ the Saviour was built in two halves,
– the line where the top fits the body can be clearly seen

The Kremlin has a double identity:
it refers to the Russian government
(or President) . . .

. . . or to the fortified cluster of
fine palaces and cathedrals

18

What the Kremlin does reflects in city life

The vast Kremlin wall reflects in puddles around the city

The fortification feature on the Kremlin walls
is known as "sparrow tails"

The Chinese pagoda style influenced the design of this bell tower in the Kremlin
- the bell, too large for the tower, houses workers

Kremlin chimneys

It's not generally known that this Kremlin outhouse . . .

. . . is actually a kennel

21

Some buildings are modelled on Russian hats, or vice versa

There are also ugly buildings,
one of the ugliest being the "Duma"
or lower house of Parliament

Pashkov House with its teapot lid
became the Lenin Library until
an ugly grey monstrosity
replaced it

Ostankino TV tower is
another dominant landmark

Friendship House is adorned with scallop shells and pearls

State airline Aeroflot also runs the bus fleets

The old English Court was England's first embassy in Russia

Старый Английский Двор
Первое посольство Англии в России
Пять веков истории

The old English Court
The First Embassy of England in Russia
Five Centuries of History

The British Ambassador's residence (formerly the British Embassy) has a prestigious site in front of the Kremlin

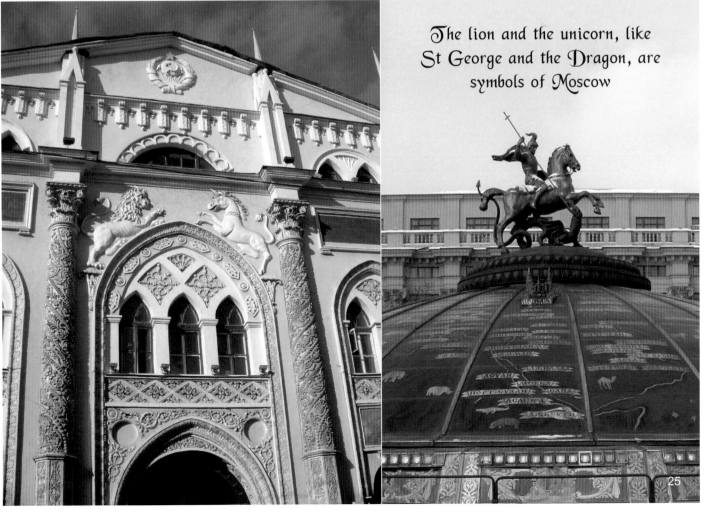

The lion and the unicorn, like St George and the Dragon, are symbols of Moscow

St George, patron saint of Moscow,
demonstrates cruelty to dragons at several locations in the capital

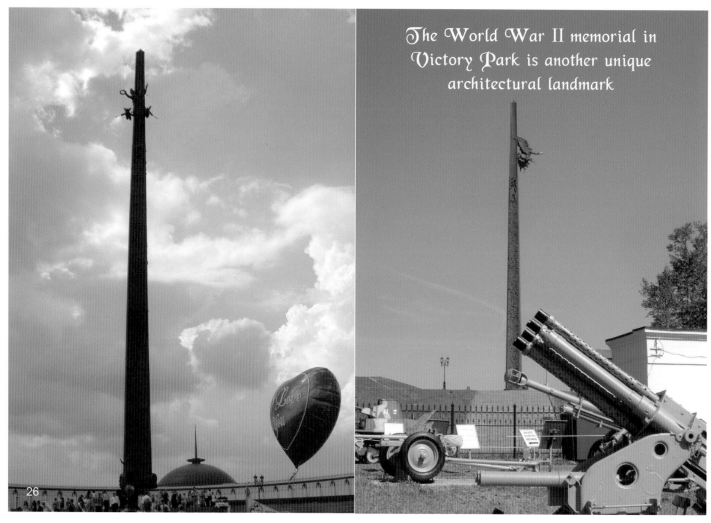

The World War II memorial in
Victory Park is another unique
architectural landmark

Stalin Skyscrapers

"Stalin skyscrapers" are monstrous layered Gothic buildings which dominate the Moscow skyline

. . . both in the grey of winter . . .

and in the summer smog

Moscow State University, one of the most imposing skyscrapers, has a garden of twisted metal flowers

Hotel Ukraina, another skyscraper, is made of gold

View of U.S. Embassy and "Barricade" apartment skyscraper from Hotel Ukraina

Some residents appreciate tall buildings

These riverside apartments give a bird's eye view of Moscow

The many faces of the Moscow river

. . . in reflective mood

. . . with a sparkle in its eye

. . . frozen and virginal

. . . unfriendly

. . . party time

Main Streets

Tverskaya is Moscow's main and busiest street

Moscow City Hall
on Tverskaya with
the city's founder
Yuri Dolgoruki

Muscovites wear fur headgear with earflaps

City Hall and the city's founder

Pushkin Square on Tverskaya is a main road and metro circus

Russian vodka brands are advertised on
Novy Arbat
– another of Moscow's busiest streets

Brooke Bond

Russian brands of vodka
are also promoted at
major landmark sites

– Revolution Square,
Central House of Artists
and even the Kremlin

КОМСОМОЛЬСКИЙ
проспект
ЛЕНИНСКИЙ пр-т
120м

Victory Arch on Kutuzovsky

*Other major streets are
Kutuzovsky to the west and
Leninsky to the south*

ОДЕЖДА
СЕКОНД ХЕНД
из США и Европы

ФОТО НА ДОКУМЕНТЫ

СИНЕМА-БАР
ПАРИКМАХЕРСКАЯ

Моя Москва - моя ЕДИНАЯ РОССИЯ!

АВТОШИНЫ

*Side streets
are also
interesting. . .*

*. . . with
character*

Martian spaceships visit central Moscow at night

. . . and sometimes by day

STATVES

Statue of Yuri Dolgoruki, founder of Moscow, with Yuri Luzhkov, mayor of Moscow, speaking – or vice versa?

Arms up, everyone!

Statues of several other Moscow heroes, such as Marshall Zhukov and General Kutuzov, are also on horseback

Statue of poet Alexander Pushkin, in Pushkin Square

Composer Tchaikovsky
outside the Moscow Conservatoire

Writer Dostoyevsky
outside the Lenin Library
with a flash-mob of pigeons

Some Soviet statues
are overgrown

Lenin on Tverskaya Square

Plinth of the statue of the invisible man

An ugly
monstrosity

(1997 statue of
Peter the Great)

40

Moscow has many bronze statues of its heroes

The well-known fable of the bear, the wolf, the fish and the duck

Stalin

Many of the Communist statues have been moved off the streets into a special statue park

Young and older Lenins
in "the Graveyard of Fallen Monuments"

KGB
founder
Dzerzhinsky

43

PARKS

Moscow has many fine parks accessible by public transport

. . . where locals and visitors can walk about

. . . and reflect on city life

Alexander Gardens
by the Kremlin . . .

. . . displays surprisingly fascist
symbols for a Communist state

. . . more surprising as Moscow's tomb of
the unknown soldier and WWII memorial
are located there

- *Bizarrely, it is customary for newly-married couples
to visit here on their wedding day*

We love Moscow

White dogs need black spots so
they can be spotted in the snow

Most of Moscow's gardens grow cabbages
for the famous Russian delicacy cabbage soup

Many of the parks and town gardens have artistic flower displays
Some also have randomly-placed coat hangers

The park of the All Union Exhibition Centre (VDNH) . . .

. . . is a sort of Soviet Disneyland

49

The park has
ornate
"pavilions"

УКРАЇНА

...and
statues
of heroes

МЯСНАЯ ПРОМЫШЛЕННОСТЬ

An oasis of tranquility
in the heart of town

51

Muscovites change the names on their houses with the seasons

They are also finding novel ways to cope with the fuel crisis

The forerunners of the Mir space station can be seen in "Disneyland"

The mobile phone transmitter masts are discreetly positioned

Buran space shuttle

Much of Russia's earlier space programme is now on display in amusement parks

The famous Gorky Park

Sokol region of Moscow also has traditional wooden houses

Yekaterina Park has traditional wooden houses

Victory Park has an interesting juxtaposition of artefacts

CHURCHES & RELIGIOUS BUILDINGS

Different religions are practised in Moscow

56

The memorial chapel in Victory Park

The Roman Catholic cathedral
is in keeping with Moscow's
Gothic-style architecture

Two of Moscow's several mosques

Ornate
Russian Orthodox
churches are
everywhere

34
СОФИЙСКАЯ

Lenin statue and chapel

60

The city is littered with pretty churches
many of which have been returned to
religious use in the last decade

In some streets
every other building is a church

Many churches are in poor repair

This courtyard beside the prestigious GUM store has a beautiful view

St Cosmos and Damian, the "Church of the Book", was the State Library of Foreign Literature

Several churches in central Moscow have recently been renovated . . .

. . . some in bright, fairground colours
and some
in pastel shades

The river docks at Fili

MUSEUMS &
ART GALLERIES

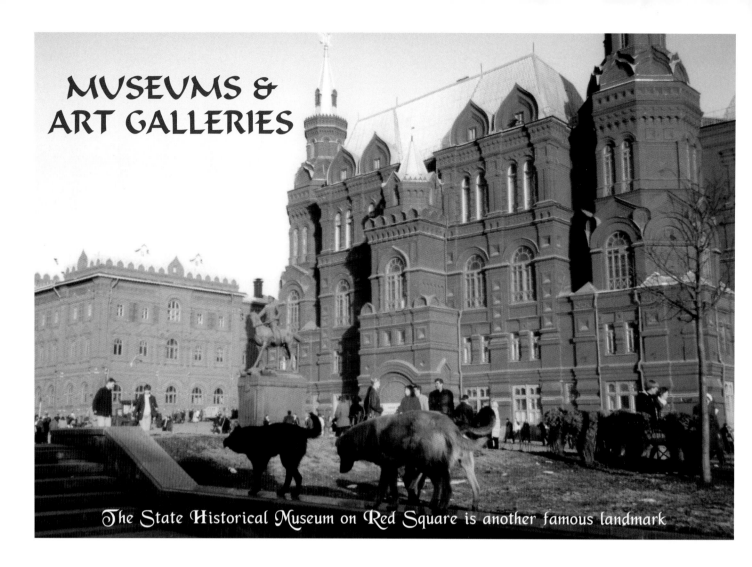

The State Historical Museum on Red Square is another famous landmark

. . . imposing from front or back

The State Historical Museum houses historical costumes, artefacts and, of course, a gourmet restaurant

Costumes for buildings are included in its collection

Museum of the Battle of Borodino: Napoleon's forces were repelled from Moscow
by troops (and fire) and the Russian winter, – both always on display outside the museum

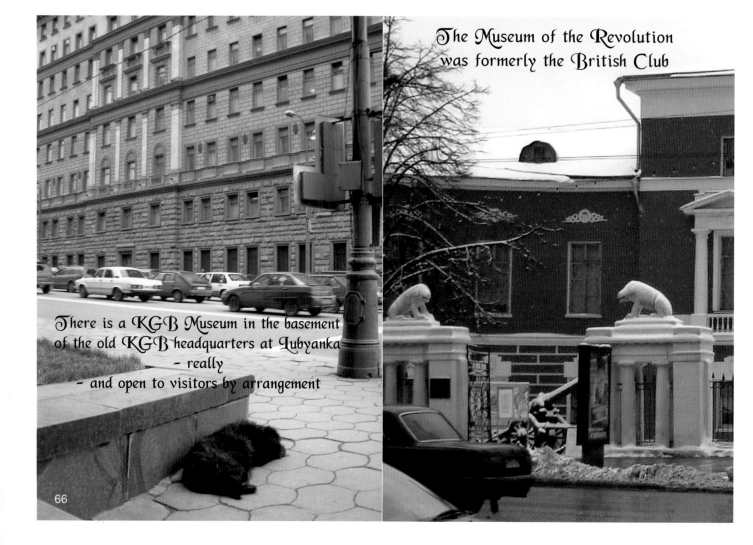

The Museum of the Revolution
was formerly the British Club

There is a KGB Museum in the basement
of the old KGB headquarters at Lubyanka
– really
– and open to visitors by arrangement

Several writers' houses are preserved as museums

Gorky's artistic house

Pushkin's colourful house

The Archaeology Museum has dug up some toilets

Believe it or not: the Gulag Museum

... a museum for all seasons ...

The War Museum ...

is one of several collections of military hardware in the heart of the city

Another is the World War II Museum . . .

. . . at Victory Park . . .

. . . displaying . . .

. . . some bizarre military equipment

A pied wagtail

A pied wagtail

Another is the Military Aircraft Museum . . .

. . . and further collections can be seen
in other museums, parks and markets around town

The recently-restored Tretyakov Gallery . . .

. . . is serious about security

The Tretyakov Gallery houses
national art treasures

Art is displayed in galleries
such as the Central House of Artists and the Pushkin Museum of Fine Art . . .

and in exhibitions . . .

. . . and on the streets

73

The world-famous Bolshoi Theatre is popular with Muscovites in summer . . .

. . . and attracts visitors
to Moscow
in winter

Theatre-goers park their vehicles
in the adjacent carpark

The Soviet Army Theatre . . .

. . . also has a car park

. . . and a
metro station

Drinking water delivered by truck is served in the interval at the Yermolova theatre

Moscow has almost as many theatres as churches . . .

Ballet is also world-famous

Both providing welcome escapism

Spectacular street theatre is
provided on special occasions

Muscovites flock to the kiosks selling tickets to concert halls . . .

. . . including the world-famous Moscow Conservatoire

Another musical hero from more recent times
(the building behind is a hospital, – no not the park hut but the one that looks like an opera house)

Playing the triangle,
Russian-style:
Balalaikas in a central
Moscow street concert

Before . . .

Balalaikas play jazz at the
Moscow Country Club

Buskers at Vernisage Market sing
"Viva España" . . .

. . . in all seasons

In the land of Tchaikovsky and Rachmaninoff, buskers and street musicians are high quality

Popular musicians performed for
Moscow's 855th birthday party

Arms up everyone!

*Traditional music can be heard anywhere that
Muscovites congregate to drink*

CITY LIFE

Kremlin workers use the adjacent park
in their lunch break

The queue for the toilets outside the Kremlin can be horrendous on busy days

Morning rush hour in central Moscow

Since the fuel crisis,
Muscovites travel on foot or by horse

More on the fuel crisis – Tverskaya Street

Most Muscovites leave town for their dachas
(small wooden summer houses) on summer weekends

Sport

The International Police Federation Olympics
take place on the square outside Moscow City Hall

Olympic events include
holding the umbrella . . .

. . . - individual and relay

. . . the wheel

. . . and storming the beer tent

Dressage

Equestrian events
take place on
Revolution Square

Football is a popular sport

As expected, Russians are keen on winter sports

Young skiers fearlessly tackle the snowy slopes of Moscow

Ice-fishing is a popular winter (in)activity

Other national pastimes include . . .

. . . chess

. . . and soliciting money

EATING OUT

A hot dog stand can provide
a packed lunch

Queues for MacDonalds are legendary. . .

. . . and entertainment is provided
for waiting customers

The ornate arches of this old monastic building on Tverskaya are used for alfresco drinking and eating by small residents

A leaking pipe provides a drink

Street cafes are popular in summer

Pushkin Square

City Hall

Kremlin Wall

Tverskaya

This typical ensemble of pastel & white architecture with oil derrick includes the upmarket restaurant Cafe Pushkin

Kamergersky Lane has several popular restaurants

Kvas, a Russian drink of fermented brown bread, is dispensed from tanks around town

The delikatessen can also provide a snack

94

SHOPPING

GUM department store on Red Square is a magnificent building . . .

. . . inside and out

The TsUM department store offers a warm welcome

. . . but fashions on offer are very traditional

. . . and shoppers are often kept hanging around

Muscovites often wear traditional dress when visiting Red Square

Yeliseev's beautiful grocery store
on Tverskaya . . .

. . . has a good deliCATessen

Street kiosks sell bread . . .

. . . and sausages

Selling watermelons on the street
is common in summer

There is little distinction between fresh
and frozen fish on the street in winter

Traditional hats are sold on the street . . .

. . . and in markets

. . . with brightly-coloured carpets

. . . and mobile phones

"I buy expensive cell phones"

Various other commodities . . .

. . . are for sale in Moscow

Toilet?

98

An icon toilet seat cover

HOTELS

The Baltschug Hotel has a commanding view of the Kremlin across the river

The Metropol with its Art Nouveau style has historical links

. . . and an exclusive clientele

The National Hotel also has an artistic mural –
and parking for alien visitors

The ugly Intourist on Tverskaya
has now been demolished

Unfortunately, the same fate is not planned
for the Rossiya

Rossiya, the least attractive building visible from Red Square,
is floodlit at night

Another grey
"Soviet Block",
the Moskva
is well located

The Slavanskaya
has its own heat &
power plant

The Russian "World Trade Centre" and
the horrendous Mezhdunarodnaya hotel

The well-known Lubyanka "hotel"
has outside toilets

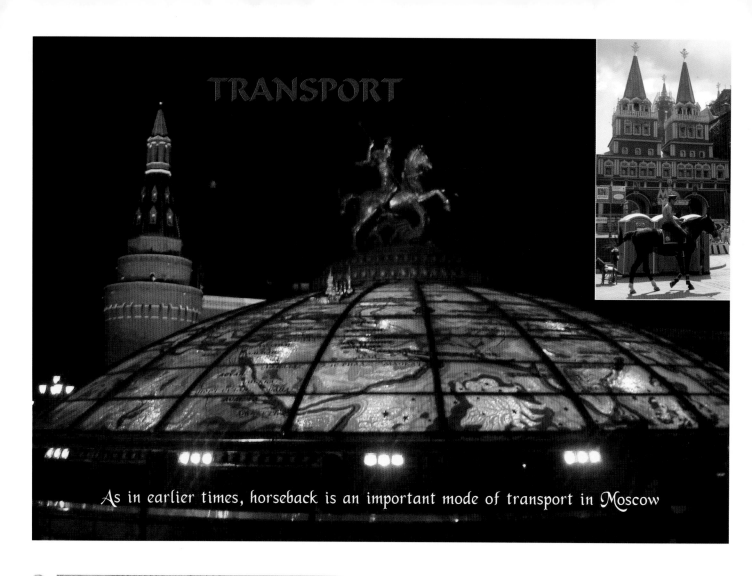

TRANSPORT

As in earlier times, horseback is an important mode of transport in Moscow

Transport around Moscow can be exciting

A town run-about

The ubiquitous white stretch limos are favoured for weddings and nights out

103

Driving conditions are tough in winter

Many Muscovites drive snowploughs whether conditions warrant it or not

Lada cars have awesome air-conditioning

Russian automotive legends: the Zil, Volga and Moskvitch

Rocket launchers are commonly parked in the city's squares

Vintage vehicles add character to the city's streets

Pollution can be bad some days

A pied wagtail

Some
roads
are
very
narrow

Foreigners park their
vehicles outside their flats

Public road transport has antlers

Buses are another way to get around the city

The French word "bistro" came from the Russian word for "quick"

The city's trains and . . .

palatial railway stations . . .

. . . are a colourful experience

Steam trains still run

Some of the trains have seen years of eventful service . . .

ЖЕЛЕЗНОДОРОЖНЫЕ ВОЙСКА
И СПЕЦФОРМИРОВАНИЯ НКПС

Эу 680-96

. . . and some are much newer

АЭРОФЛОТ

СССР-85005

Railway terminals are "palaces of the people"

Belorussky railway station
– exterior and interior

ПРИГОРОДНЫЕ КАССЫ

Kievsky railway
station

Another steam train

Kazansky railway station

The famous Moscow metro has varied architectural styles . . .

. . . for its exterior buildings

111

The metro is used by . . .

. . . millions of travellers each day

It is an artistic experience . . .

. . . with hallways like palaces, and paintings, mosaics and sculptures

Mayakovskaya ceiling mosaics

114

Despite the artwork, travelling is very tiring

Park Pobedy metro opened in 2003

The metro is an efficient way to travel

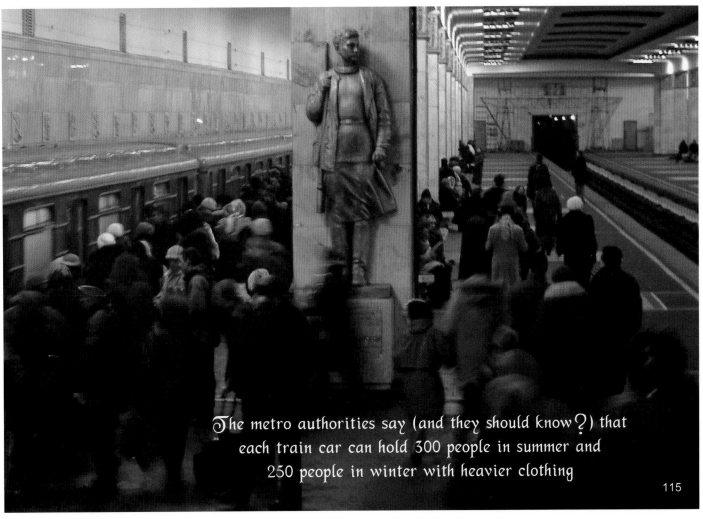

The metro authorities say (and they should know?) that
each train car can hold 300 people in summer and
250 people in winter with heavier clothing

Travelling by boat on the River Moscow
is an alternative and scenic option

Reflect on the views

Many types of vessel
are available

Some boats are stranded
when the river runs dry

In addition to bridges,
a ferry crosses the River Moscow in front of the Kremlin

North river terminal

A visitor arriving at Moscow's north river terminal is met by a friend

(I lived on this boat - Konstantin Fedin - in Kazan for a week in 1994; this picture taken Moscow 2001)

117

Moscow has several airports convenient for the city centre

With, of course, an airport car park . . .

. . . where your car may be raided
for parts for aircraft use

The car park caters for all types of vehicle

. . . and the city is not far from the airfields

118

Another way to see Moscow is from the air

The town and surrounding countryside can
be seen from many angles . . .

119

. . . in different types of aircraft

Around Moscow are picturesque towns such as Kolomna

As in much of Asia, the flying carpet is as common a mode of transport as the car, and vehicle showrooms, like this one at Izmailovsky Park, cater for both

There are several other ways to get around Moscow and to enjoy the sights of this remarkable city

A Foreign View of Moscow

This is an assortment of personal
photographs of the City of Moscow,
from a visitor's perspective,
intentionally focusing on public buildings
and public places rather than on individual
people and private lives and homes.

The darker, crueller side of city life,
amply evident on the streets daily,
has also deliberately been excluded
from this collection.

No animals were harmed or distressed
in collecting these pictures.

The captions are intended to add
interest or humour; they are
not intended to mislead or to offend.

Thank you, Moscow, for the good times
and the bad; there were many of both.